Aural Time!

Practice Tests for the New Revised ABRSM Syllabus and Other Exams

Grade 8

DAVID TURNBULL

CONTENTS

Published by
Bosworth & Co. Limited
14-15 Berners Street,
London W1T 3LJ, UK.

Exclusive Distributors:
Music Sales Limited
Distribution Centre, Newmarket Road,
Bury St Edmunds, Suffolk IP33 3YB, UK.
Music Sales Pty Limited
20 Resolution Drive, Caringbah,
NSW 2229, Australia.

This book © Copyright 2010 Bosworth.
International Copyright Secured.

Printed in the EU.

BOSWORTH
part of The Music Sales Group

INTRODUCTION

Having had the privilege of working with the late David Turnbull on a number of his projects, including the original publication of some of the *Aural Time!* volumes, it is a great pleasure to contribute to this new edition of his work, which takes account of various mainly small revisions to the aural tests of the Associated Board of the Royal Schools of Music examinations, effective from January 2011 onwards.

At Grade 8 the only significant change is in Test A (iii) where the number of chords to be identified is now limited to three – a single approach chord followed by the final two chords of the cadence.

The approach to Test D in Grade 8 is a little different to that in the earlier grades, as the examiner will invite candidates to describe notable features of the piece rather than asking them specific questions (although the examiner will prompt with questions if the candidate gets stuck). Possible subjects for discussion are shown beneath the music examples in Section D of this book – it is not expected that candidates will talk about every element listed, but they should aim to mention as many points as possible. Pupils should be encouraged to use technical terms in their answers, and should aim to support any subjective statements by referring to specific features of the music. For example, a statement that the piece has a mournful character could be evidenced by mentioning its minor key, slow tempo and thick, chordal texture. Similarly, any view on the period of the music should be supported by evidence. For instance, in the case of a 20th-century work, this might be the use of angular melodies, free metre and dissonant harmonies.

As with the rest of the *Aural Time!* series, David Turnbull took most of the examples from the works of established composers. However, in many cases they have been adapted or transposed to make them more useful for their present purpose. This is particularly true of examples which have to be sung.

Paul Terry
London, 2010

Uniform with this volume: *Aural Time!* Grades 1–7.

Also by David Turnbull: *Theory Time!* Step-by-step instruction in musical theory and rudiments. Grades 1–5.

All published by Bosworth & Co.

Test 8A

There are **three sections** to this test.

i. The pupil must *sing or play from memory* the *lowest* part of a three-part phrase (marked ⎣____⎦) played twice. Before each playing the key-chord and starting note must be played and named, and the pulse indicated.

ii. The pupil must *name* the cadence at the end of a second (following) phrase as perfect, plagal, imperfect or interrupted. This second phrase must be played *twice*, preceded each time by its key-chord.

iii. The key-chord must be sounded once more, and the three chords (marked *) played. These must then be played a second time, **with a pause on each**, so that the pupil can name the chords. The chords which may be used are:

   the tonic (root position, first inversion or second inversion);
   the supertonic (root position or first inversion);
   the subdominant (root position);
   the dominant (root position, first inversion or second inversion);
   the dominant seventh (root position);
   the submediant (root position).

Chords may be described as above, or by using Roman numerals with an indication of the chord's position (e.g. Vb) or by using letter names (e.g. C major, first inversion).

4

CD Tracks 32–34

CD Tracks 35–37

CD Tracks 38–40

6

Test B. Sight-Singing

Pupils must sing at sight the lower part of a two-part passage, the upper part being played for them by the teacher or examiner. The passage can be in any major or minor key up to and including those with four sharps or four flats. The key-chord and the starting note will be played, and the pulse indicated.

In examinations, candidates may choose to sing a passage in *either* the treble *or* the bass clef. **In practice sessions pupils are strongly advised to use both clefs, to increase their familiarity with them.**

In examinations, a second attempt may be allowed (although this will affect the assessment). When practising, pupils should repeat the test as often as necessary to get a correct performance.

10

Test C. Modulations.

In Grade 7, pupils learned to recognise modulations from a major key to the keys of its dominant, subdominant and relative minor. In addition to these, at Grade 8 pupils must be able to recognise modulations from a minor key to its dominant, subdominant or relative major.

In examinations, two different passages will be played, the first starting in a major key and the second in a minor key. Each will be played once, and the examiner will name and play the tonic chord of the starting key.

Candidates should answer either by giving the relationship of the new key to the opening key (e.g. dominant) or by stating the name of the new key (e.g. F major).

Note that a passage in a minor key might modulate to either the dominant major or dominant minor, but in either case it is only necessary to recognise that the new key is the dominant.

It may be helpful for pupils to practise these preliminary exercises, by C. H. Kitson. Pupils should listen to them, and if possible play them over – if pupils are not keyboard players, recommend them to sing or play each part over separately.

CD Track 57
Poco allegro

Bach

1

CD Track 58
Allegro

Mozart

2

CD Track 59
Allegretto

Beethoven

3

Allegretto

Glinka

4

Allegro vivace

Donizetti

5

14

Test D. Discussing musical features

The approach to Test D in Grade 8 is somewhat different from that adopted in the earlier grades, in which questions were asked about specific musical features of a short piece of music.

In Grade 8, the examiner will simply ask candidates to describe the features they notice in the music that will be played to them. The examiner will only ask more specific questions if the candidate needs some prompting. Pupils should be encouraged to discuss at least three of the following areas as fluently as possible, depending on what seems important in the piece concerned, using technical terminology where appropriate:

Rhythm (including Tempo);
Melody;
Tonality;
Dynamics;
Articulation;
Harmony;
Texture;
Structure;
Style and period.

Examples from Test D sections, with their notes, in *Aural Time!* Grades 6 and 7 can be used for further practice.

The skills learnt to tackle Test D will be of great use to pupils in other examinations, such as A-level Music, as well as in their musical development as a whole, and the general approach to analytical discussion is a skill that can be transferred to fields other than music.

Brief comments about the music in this section will be found below each example. *Pupils should be reminded that these comments and opinions are not the only possible ones. They may wish to add others of their own, but must always be prepared to justify their comments with evidence from the music.*

CD Track 74

[**Andantino**]

Chopin

D1 (Chopin: *Cantabile in B♭ major*). Possible subjects for discussion include:

Tempo	A gentle andante, with some rubato. In last line, a *rallentando* and a dying away.
Melodic phrases	First phrase concludes with an imperfect cadence; a modified repeat of this ends with a perfect cadence. The rest of the piece is a coda over a tonic pedal, consisting of a shorter phrase, repeated, rounded off by tonic chords decorated with appoggiaturas.
Articulation	Legato and *cantabile* melodic line until the final chords.
Dynamics	Use of *cresc.* and *dim.* throughout. Coda very soft and dies away at the end.
Tonality and Harmony	Major key and essentially without modulation – but there are many secondary 7ths and other **chromatic** chords. Final section (last 6 bars) has a **tonic pedal**.
Texture	Homophonic: the free and expressive melodic line supported by steady left-hand broken chords spanning a wide range is characteristic of a **Nocturne**.

All these features suggest piano music of the Romantic period, particularly Chopin.

CD Track 75

D2 (Byrd: *Victoria*). Possible subjects for discussion include:

Form	Two sections of equal length. The second is a **variation** of the first.
Metre	Simple triple, with **hemiola** (e.g. bars 6–7) and **syncopation** (bars 5 and 8).
Tempo	Consistent steady pulse. The second section seems faster than the first because of the **divisions** of the beats.
Melodic phrases	Mainly conjunct. Long notes in the first section. The second half is a variation of the first, using much shorter note lengths.
Dynamics	All at the same level.
Tonality, etc.	Major key: both sections modulate to the subdominant, and from there straight to the dominant.
Harmony	Mostly triads in root-position and first position. Suspensions at the cadences in the first section and many inessential notes in the second section.
Texture	Mainly homophonic, but some contrapuntal movement in the tenor part of the second section.

The lack of contrast in the dynamics, the triadic harmony and the way in which chords of long duration are decorated suggest keyboard music (for Virginals or Harpsichord) of the late Renaissance or early Baroque period.

CD Track 76

Sehr langsam

Liszt

D3 (Liszt: No. 3 of *Four Little Piano Pieces*). Possible subjects for discussion include:

Tempo A slow tempo, with *ritardandi* and pauses at the end of the second and final sections.

Form Ternary. An opening phrase, repeated with modification to cadence in the dominant. Middle section based on the falling figure from this cadence. Final section similar to first, but with thicker texture and change of key.

Articulation Legato throughout.

Dynamics Quiet, but with some modification at the end of the central section.

Tonality, etc. Major, with modulations to related keys. There is an unexpected modulation (a **tertiary** modulation – here, up a major 3rd from F♯ to A major) at the start of the final section but this ends back in the tonic key.

Harmony Mostly diatonic harmony but notice the diminished 7th that ends the central section.

Texture It starts with a homophonic two-part texture, in thirds and sixths, then progressively thickens. The middle section is imitative.

Character Contemplative, almost like church music.

The changes in tempo, use of sustaining pedal, pause on a diminished 7th and tertiary modulation suggest piano music of the Romantic period.

Stravinsky

D4 (Stravinsky: No. 1 from *Les Cinq Doigts*). Possible subjects for discussion include:

Melody	Narrow range, with some feeling of folksong. Mostly **conjunct**, but a rising 4th is a feature of the middle section.
Rhythm	Simple: no dotted notes, syncopation or irregular patterns.
Metre	Simple duple, but with a single bar of triple metre in the first (and last) section.
Form	Ternary, with exact repeat of A section.
Dynamics	No variety.
Tonality, etc.	Major; entirely diatonic.
Harmony	Non-functional **diatonic harmony** with frequent dissonance. Middle section is based on a dominant pedal.
Texture	Mostly two- and three-part homophonic, but with a little independence of parts later. The entire piece uses a relatively high texture.

The constant use of unprepared dissonance suggests early twentieth century piano music.

Allegro moderato

Grieg

con Pedale

D5 (Grieg: *Poetic Tone Picture* Op.3 No. 5, first section). Possible subjects for discussion include:

Phrase structure	The extract consists of two musical sentences. The first consists of a phrase (bars 1-4) that is repeated in **sequence** (bars 5-8) a third lower. The second is a varied restatement of the first, starting louder and with a short extension to end in the tonic.
Tempo and rhythm	A fast speed, with a *rit.* at the end of the extract. The accompaniment, in particular, features **syncopation**.
Dynamics	Contrasted: a quiet start and end, but a loud restatement of the main theme in the middle.
Articulation	Particularly strong accents on the first beats of some of the bars.
Tonality	Major key, with some **chromaticism** (particularly at phrase endings).
Harmony	7ths, 9ths, chromatic chords and short pedal points help make the harmony quite complex.
Texture	Predominantly chordal and quite thick: in the second half the bass is mainly an octave lower and the open fifths (now with crushed notes) are more prominent.

The rich harmony, chromaticism, syncopation and frequent use of the sustaining pedal all suggest piano music of the Romantic period.

D6 (Beethoven: Bagatelle, Op. 119 No, 11). Possible subjects for discussion include:

Form and Texture	Two *cantabile* sections, separated by a two-bar link, and concluded with a short coda. The first section has a repeated four-bar melody, supported by simple chords, followed by a two-bar phrase in similar style and texture which is then repeated up a tone in free **sequence**. The second section has a new four-bar melody, sounded high on the piano with a chordal accompaniment. This is repeated an octave lower with much greater independence of parts. The four-bar coda is strictly **homophonic**.

Dynamics	Predominantly *p* but with some variation.
Tonality	Major, with brief modulations to related keys in the second half of the first section only.
Harmony	Straightforward, **functional** harmony. The diatonic opening is built around an inner **pedal** on the dominant. A diminished 7th introduces the chromatic link.
Character	Restrained and contemplative. The outer sections are almost hymn-like, but the diminished 7th heralds a change of mood to legato melody contrasting with detached accompaniment.
	The functional harmony and periodic phrasing point to the Classical style, with some romantic elements. Early 19th Century in period.

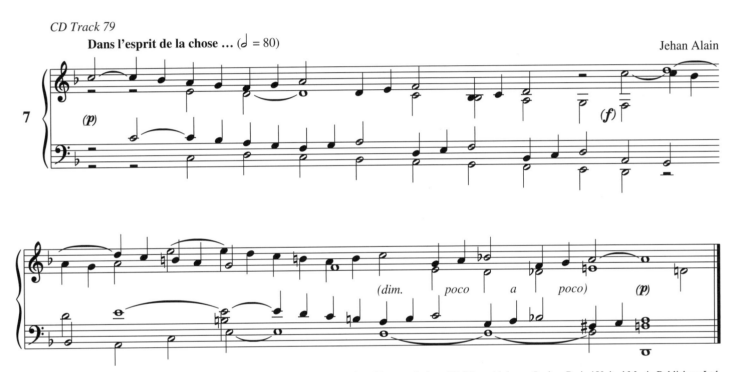

CD Track 79

Dans l'esprit de la chose ... (♩ = 80)

Jehan Alain

7 (*p*) (*f*)

(*dim.* *poco* *a* *poco*) (*p*)

Reproduced by permission of Editions Alphonse Leduc, Paris / United Music Publishers Ltd.

D7 (Jehan Alain: *En dévissant mes chaussettes*, No. 9 of *Dix Pièces pour Piano*, 1931). Possible subjects for discussion include:

Metre	No fixed metre to this piece (it is **ametric**, or 'in free time'), but it flows continuously.
Melody	Mainly descending scales with an even crotchet (quarter note) rhythm that permeates almost the entire piece. (The bass has a long descending scale in minims).
Texture	Basically four-part counterpoint, with **canonic imitation** between treble and tenor voices.
Dynamics	Piano at the start, a small climax at the forte in the middle, and dying away to a piano end.
Tempo	No change other than (possibly) a slight *rit.* at the end.
Tonality, etc.	The lack of conventional cadences gives the music a modal quality, although there is a feeling of tonal centres that progress from major to relative minor through the course of the piece. The ending is tonally ambiguous, with a chromatic chord and major-minor conflict over a tonic pedal.
	The metrical freedom, modality and diatonic dissonance (together with tonally ambiguous ending), suggest an early Twentieth Century date.

Pachelbel

D8 (Pachelbel: Fugue). Possible subjects for discussion include:

Texture & form	A four-voice **fugue**, although the contrapuntal texture is often in just two or three parts.
Dynamics	No change in the level of dynamic (other than that caused by differences in texture).
Tempo	No change other than (possibly) a slight *rit.* at the end.
Tonality, etc.	Major key, with brief modulations to nearly-related keys only. There is a very short chromatic passage in the middle.
Rhythm	Constant driving pulse of short note-lengths, with much repetition of rhythmic patterns.
	The fugal texture, **monothematicism** (use of a single theme) and driving rhythm all suggest Baroque keyboard music.

D9 (Hanns Jelinek: *Charakterstiick* from *Zwölftonwerk*, Op. 15/2). Possible subjects for discussion include:

Melodic shape	Angular (**disjunct** motion), with wide leaps in many places.
Form	An arch form, in which a central climax is differentiated by dynamic, texture, pitch range and articulation. The opening material re-appears in free inversion in the last three bars.
Texture	Two-part texture throughout. The treble and bass are in **dialogue** for most of the piece, coming together briefly at the central climax.

(continued on page 28)

Dynamics	A long crescendo from the start to the central climax, and then a quiet ending. There is wide variation in the dynamic level.
Articulation	Legato (distubed by off-beat accents) in the outer sections; heavily accented at the climax.
Tempo	Quite fast, but with frequent changes (fastest at the central climax).
Tonality, etc.	**Atonal** (no fixed key centre) and therefore not in any major or minor scale. (Actually dodecaphonic though a pupil would be unlikely to gasp this on one hearing.)
Harmony	Dissonant in many places.
	The dissonance and extremes of expression suggest a mid-Twentieth Century date.

CD Track 82

[Grave]

Bach

10

D10 (Bach: Prelude, BWV 931). Possible subjects for discussion include:

Texture	Mainly three-part writing: the bass has considerable contrapuntal independence but the two top parts are often in parallel thirds. There is significant ornamentation in all parts.
Dynamics	No change in the level of dynamics.
Tempo	A steady pulse, which doesn't change other than (possibly) a slight *rit.* at the end.
Tonality, etc.	Minor key, but with a **tierce de picardie** at the end, so it finishes on a major *chord*. There are brief modulations in the central part of the piece.
Harmony	Basically simple chords are highly decorated with suspensions and appoggiaturas.
	The contrapuntal texture, along with the melodic and harmonic decoration, suggest keyboard music of the late Baroque, and particularly Bach.

CD Track 83

D11 (Haydn: Minuet from Sonata in F.) Possible subjects for discussion include:

Form	**Binary** form minuet. The B section is longer than the A section and begins with a variant of the opening melody, transferred to the bass.
Melody	The main theme is characterised by an upward leap followed by a descending scale. This two-bar phrase is repeated in **sequence** and then answered by a four-bar phrase modulating to the dominant. The entire piece is constructed from similarly regular (**periodic**) phrases. Generally, the melody has a wide range and is frequently decorated.
Texture	Thin, melody-dominated texture, often in just two parts.
Dynamics	No changes in the level of dynamics.
Tempo and Rhythm	A steady pulse. All phrases are characterised by an up-beat (**anacrusic**) start.
Tonality, etc.	Major key, modulating to the dominant in the middle.
Harmony	**Functional** harmony, with a little chromatic decoration and a number of suspensions and appoggiaturas.
	The melody-dominated texture, functional harmony, periodic phrasing and melodic decoration all suggest a minuet in the Classical style.

D12 (Rameau: first part of *Tambourin* from Pièces de Clavecin, 1724) Possible subjects for discussion include:

Form	**Rondo**: three refrains separated by two quieter episodes (ABACA).
Melody	The refrain consists of two nearly identical phrases, differing only in that the first ends with an imperfect cadence while the second ends with a perfect cadence. The melody of the first episode is similar to the refrain, but it begins an octave higher. The melody of the second episode is **chromatic**. Ornamentation with **mordents** occurs throughout.
Texture	Melody with chordal accompaniment.
Dynamics	Sharply contrasted by section (**terraced** dynamics).
Tempo and Rhythm	Fast, duple time and regular phrase lengths suggesting a dance movement: the rhythmic structure is that of a **gavotte**.
Tonality, etc.	Minor key, without modulation, but with a chromatic passage in the second episode.
Harmony	Almost entirely tonic and dominant chords, apart from the chromatic section. There is a tonic **pedal** throughout (a double pedal, or drone bass, in the A and B sections).

The driving rhythm, simple harmony, terraced dynamics, monothematicism and constant ornamentation all suggest a *gavotte en rondeau* in the French Baroque style.